Prayers for Young People

# DAVID GATWARD

# Leaving Home

Kevin Mayhew

First published in 1996 by
KEVIN MAYHEW LTD
Rattlesden
Bury St Edmunds
Suffolk IP30 0SZ



ISBN 0 86209 829 7
Catalogue No 1500065

0 1 2 3 4 5 6 7 8 9

Cover illustration by Roy Mitchell

Design by Veronica Ward
Artwork by Graham Johnstone

Edited by Peter Dainty
Typesetting by Louise Hill
Printed and bound in Great Britain

# Contents


| | |
|---|---|
| Lord, Are You There? | 5 |
| No Chance! | 8 |
| On the Platform | 11 |
| My New Room | 14 |
| Missing Home | 18 |
| Drowning | 22 |
| Thrown Out! | 24 |
| To Boldly Go! | 27 |

# Lord, Are You There?

Lord, are you there?
It's just that I'm on my own
and I need someone to talk to.
(You don't mind if we have a chat,
do you, Lord?)
I've just moved out, left home.
It's kind of strange really.
You can't go downstairs
and expect someone to be there,
watching TV
and ready for a chat.
There's no vast pool of friends to call on.
The church is strange.
People are strange.
You're suddenly on your own.
You say to yourself, 'It'll be fine'.
Convince yourself nothing
can shake you.
Tell your family,
'Don't worry, I'll be OK.'
I'm not saying I'm depressed, Lord,
or totally friendless or lonely.
It's just that it's a bit of a shock
to the system.

It's so weird being away from home.
I keep running the fact I've left home
over and over in my mind.

How did you feel when you left home, Lord?

Did you feel lonely?

Lord, this brings up the thought
of your call to us.
You said we have to leave our families
and take up our cross and follow you.
Do you know how hard that is, Lord?
My family mean so much to me.
They've helped me so much.
And my friends have too.
Some of them are so very special.
I can't cope if I lose touch with them.
My social life,
my hobbies,
my life.
Lord, don't you think it's too
much to ask?
To give up everything for you?
How can I, Lord?
How?

'David, listen to me!
I gave up everything.
I was rejected in my home town.
I was betrayed by one of
  my closest friends.
I was denied three times.
They couldn't even stay awake for me.
And then I died, David.
I died for you.
I died so that you could know me.
I will never leave you, David.
I will always be by your side.
Because I love you
  I ask you to follow me.'

Amen.

## No Chance!

What are we here for? What a question! It's baffled and occupied some of the greatest minds since the dawn of time, and so I'm not going to add to the masterpieces of literature and philosophy with a rundown of my own pet theories. Wouldn't it be great though, if when we were born there could be a little note pinned on us by the Creator, saying 'This one is here to be a writer', or it could be musician, mechanic, nurse, accountant, brickie, whatever. It would solve a lot of problems, knowing what we are actually here for, what we've got to do, and which direction in life we need to take.

Unfortunately, it's not that easy, but then, God never intended life to be as dull and uninteresting as that would make it! Instead he gives us guides – indicators to follow and to use to get our bearings. Through prayer, reading the Bible, listening to people we trust and so on, the way ahead can start to become clear. We might make a wrong turn here and there, but I can't believe that God has only one possible plan for our lives and that if we get it wrong we've fouled things up for good. It doesn't work like that.

When we do go wrong, providing we recognise it and ask for his help, he sorts us out, brushes us down, makes sure any cuts and bruises are dealt with, and then he sets us back on the path. Because of what we've done, or failed to do, the path may now take a different turn, but he's adapted his purposes and given us a new plan to follow. The important thing is to trust him, and to follow him. The way ahead may never seem easy or even appealing, but he'll never allow it to test us beyond our capabilities, and we can always guarantee it will be stimulating, challenging and fulfilling. Believing that, who wants it to be easy?

Lord, I hope you don't mind
  me asking, but . . .
Has anything of any use come from me?
Look at me. I'm a waste of space, really.
Mixed-up ideas. Crazy views.
As screwed-up, weird,
  and strange as you'll ever get.
So, what use am I?

I know you've got a really good
   sense of humour, Lord,
   but I'm beginning to feel I'm the one
   who doesn't get the joke
   when everyone around me is laughing!
What is my purpose?
My reason for being here?
I wish you'd tell me.
I'm really wanting to believe in you, trust you.
But right now I just can't see where
   it's getting me.
Can't you give me a hint
   as to the direction I need to take?
Somewhere it says that you're the potter
   and we're the clay.
So how about it, Lord?
I'm tired of being the sticky lump
   on the potter's wheel.
I want to move on,
   become what you want me to be.
So that when I look
   and wonder if anything good
   will come from me,
   you'll be able to show me that it already has.

Amen.

# On the Platform

Well, Lord, this is it . . . the big step.
I'm off to Uni.
Doesn't seem to be real to be honest,
  standing here, suitcase and guitar in hand,
  tickets in my pocket, one way . . .
Is this happening?

I remember sitting at home, choosing.
Where do I go?
What do I want to do?
And Lord, I'm still pretty unsure.
Everyone else appears to know where they
  are going, and why they are going there.
Yet I seem to be more confused
  about which platform I should be on.
(This is the right one isn't it, Lord?
  You've a better view than me.)

Where am I going, Lord?
I remember the visiting day, the interview,
  massive buildings, people everywhere.
It felt like being back at primary school,
  that first day, clutching my bag,
  footsteps echoing down the corridor

which towered above me,
all the other children looking,
staring at the new boy,
led into a room of strangers.

And now, a few years on,
I'm back there, in that corridor, with my bag . . .
eighteen years down the road
and everything I own and need in one bag;
odd that; leaving so much behind –
all the unnecessaries –
kneeling on the floor of my room
deciding what to leave,
what to take:
photos of friends, of family; tapes, CDs.
(. . . and that teddy I was given when
I was one – but don't tell anybody.)

I don't feel prepared.

I should be.
I've worked for this;
passed my exams . . . sort of . . .
all to get here, to this platform,
this little piece of tarmac that I'll soon step off
on to a train going one way,

away from home, family,
places I know, places I grew up with,
to a place which is new, alien, unexplored,
exciting, frightening, full of questions.
Will I cope?
Will I understand?
What's the beer like?
Will I know where the toilets are?
(. . . and will I be able to find them in the middle
of the night, in the dark with a hangover?)

Here's the train, Lord.
This is it.
Once my feet are on board, I'm off.
Pick up my life in a bag and on to that train.
Sit next to someone I don't know.
Watch childhood places whizz past the window;
allowing myself to be taken to that big
new place with the long dark corridors,
strange faces and funny smells,
as I clutch my bag and step into a new world.

Lord . . .
Hold my hand . . .

Amen.

## My New Room

I'm here,
   in my new room,
   in the college I chose,
   sitting on my bed,
   staring at the pink walls,
   the sounds of strangers
   filtering through under the door,
   strangers who will soon become friends
   as our, until now separate,
   lives connect.

Faces that I've never seen,
   I'll recognise.

Voices that I've never heard,
   I'll listen to.

So I just thought that I'd sit here,
   on my own, and settle a bit,
   in my new room . . .

My new room.
It's an odd place, Lord.
It feels a bit like a prison cell crossed with

a hospital ward;
small, cold,
full of stuff that is mine to use
for the duration:
two beds, two desks, two wardrobes
and a sink.

Not exactly four star,
not exactly home.

The carpet's worn.
The paint is chipped.
The taps are leaking.

Nice curtains though; nice and brown.
Well, brown in the places that aren't
see-through.

This bed is terrible:
three springs, all in the middle.
(Maybe I'll take the other one,
seeing as my room-mate isn't here yet.)

It is hard to believe,
that this small, four sided,
rabbit hutch sized room is now my home.

Home used to be where there was
a bathroom that was warm,
a front room with an open fire,
a garden at the back,
family to talk to,
dogs to take for a walk.

Now it is this.

The bathroom is at the end of the corridor.
The floors are sticky and the showers
already have mud in them.
A common room with a pool table,
coke machine,
condom machine and bar
A piece of grass in the courtyard that hasn't
been mown for at least three months, and
people to talk to that I haven't even met yet.

Home.
My new room.

I remember getting my own room
for the first time at home;
my own room for my own things,
a place for me, my space.

And now it's in reverse.

My new room is also someone else's new room:
a someone else with fears, anxieties,
apprehensions;
a someone with stories to tell;
a someone who will share my time, my life;
a stranger who will become a friend; a mate.
In the new room which to us both is
'My new room'.

And Lord,
in this, my new room,
I speak to you in the silence
of my uncertainty
as I sit in the anticipation of
the next part of my life;
a part I have chosen to follow,
a part I have no map for.

Guide me . . .
in this, my new room.

Amen.

# Missing Home

Lord,
I've got to college, passed all the grades,
settled in, made friends,
handed in an essay or two (honest);
and now, sitting here on my own,
I miss my home, my family, my friends.
I'm happy here, Lord.
It's just that every now and again
I get a twinge, a pulling inside,
and my mind drifts back along that road,
the road home.

The oddest thing of all though, Lord,
is that it isn't the big things you miss,
but the small:
the way that my bedroom door
always creaked;
that dodgy floor board that gave me
away on so many late nights.

Why miss that?

The chill in the bathroom, early morning,
when dad had left the window open all night;

no hot water left, thanks to my brother
spending about three days in the shower;

the smell of home-made bread hitting
your nose as you walk into the house;
a log fire crackling and laughing in the
hearth in the front room;

rain on the window on a Sunday afternoon;
Dad under the bonnet of his precious
Range Rover;
the two dogs sitting at your feet as you
eat your tea watching *Cartoon Time* on
a Saturday evening;

late night suppers with my brothers,
when we cleared mum out of all the
bread, cheese and peanut butter;
musical instruments echoing from one
or more rooms, trying their hardest to
sound 'good';

walking on an evening down the street
to the local newsagents to buy an extra
pint of milk; nipping to the chippy;
going out with a few friends.

I miss it, Lord.
I miss it all and more.
But I have to move on.

I'm twenty-one, yet I feel eleven.
I'm that same child in an older, bigger body.
I still want to run in the woods,
  sit in front of the fire eating my tea,
  get toys for Christmas
  and believe in Santa Claus.

But I can't; or so people tell me.
'You're grown up now!' they say.
'Act your age!'

But Lord,
  I don't want my age to dictate my
  behaviour or how old people say I
  should act.
  I want it to be me; how old I am inside.

You said that if we couldn't be like little
  children we wouldn't get into heaven.

And that, Lord, is, I believe, one of the most
  important things you said.

We should not forget our childhood days,
leave them behind,
act 'grown up' – they are a part of us.
We are all children at heart.

We all still need to be as a child:
to hold a parent's hand,
run through leaves in autumn,
wander through imaginary worlds in
our minds
and dream . . .

So, Lord,
sitting here,
I remember my childhood home.
I dream of sitting by that fire on a
Saturday afternoon
watching TV,
the dogs beside me
and a glass of lemonade in my hand.

I miss my home, Lord,

and I'm glad.

Amen.

## Drowning

Lord,
I'm lost.
I've come so far and now I've lost my direction.
I thought coming to college was a good idea:
further my education,
increase my chances for employment,
have a laugh for a few years.
But I can't help wondering if I've made the
wrong choice.

I guess you're tired of hearing this one:
students tired of their lot, confused, lost,
undecided as to the meaning of their life.

Well, I'm another of them,
one of the many, no doubt;
sick of the system,
tired of the teaching,
yearning to experience life outside the
classroom, see the real world,
leave behind pointless essays
on irrelevant subjects,
taught by lecturers
who have never lived in a real world,

in an institution existing only
for its own self-gratification.

I don't want this.

I'm swimming towards an island which I
created that doesn't exist anymore;
an island sitting in a sea of questions
that float unanswered;
an island that holds the dreams
that I've forgotten;
ideals that I've mislaid,
futures I've wished for
and watched float over the horizon.
I'm swimming, Lord,
but I'm beginning to sink.

I'm tired, Lord,
and all I want is to stop,
let everything wash over me as I sink to the
bottom and drift without a care.

Hold my head above the water, Lord.
Don't let me drown.

Amen.

## Thrown Out!

Lord, I've just been thrown out, asked to leave.
'Don't come back . . .'

Not college.
The house I live in – well . . . lived in.

The landlord asked to see me.
'Nothing personal,' he said, but it would be
preferable . . . if I didn't come back.

It's funny really,
I've only been here for six weeks.
Most of the time I'm out.
My room's fairly tidy . . . (honest . . .)

Yet I've been asked to leave.
So now I've nowhere to call home except
where my parents live,
. . . three hundred miles away.
I could commute . . . by aeroplane.

Perhaps not.
I guess I'll just have to start looking for
somewhere else.

The thing is though, Lord, I'm still rather
  confused as to why I have been thrown out!

Do I smell?
  (I shower . . . well, most days!)
Do I have wild parties?
  (Yes . . . in other people's houses!)
Do I play loud music at unsociable hours?
  (No . . . my stereo is bust!)
Do I walk rudely into other people's rooms
  and rummage through their stuff?
Do I walk up the stairs too loudly?!

WHY HAVE I BEEN THROWN OUT??
I guess I can cope with it, Lord.
I find it quite funny really.
In some ways I wish I *had* had all those
  wild parties!
At least to have a couple of real reasons
  for being thrown out!

But, Lord,
  what must it be like to be thrown out
  if you've missed your rent payments?
  If your house has been repossessed?
Where do you go then?

What if you don't have a family –
  where do you go then?
Is there anywhere to go?

There should be
  government funded hostels,
  somewhere to go while you sort it out,
  a place where help is freely available.

But I can't help wondering, Lord,
  that it isn't there; that people are left out in the cold, thrown out, cast out,
  living amongst the rubbish on our streets.

I've been thrown out, Lord.
But I've somewhere to go;
  people who'll help me.
I'm not alone.

Help me to remember that and to remember
  those others who have found themselves thrown out, but without warning, those on our streets, alone.
Sit by them, Lord.

Amen.

# To Boldly Go!

Lord,
this is Student David J. Gatward of the
bedroom 'Slobberprise'.
My voyage . . .
to explore strange new fungus
inside coffee mugs,
to meet new levels of dribbling,
gigglesome inebriation,
and to boldly go . . .

Er . . . Lord?
You got a minute?

This 'boldly going' business.
Do I have to?
You see it's rather comfortable down here
at the moment.
I have everything I need
or could ever want,
(except that racing green convertible TVR
Chimaera that I mentioned last night),

So why does the world demand
that I get up and go somewhere?

I don't really want to.

It's nice here:
pub just up the road,
great friends,
laughs,
late mornings,
good food (except when you know
who's cooked it . . .),
relaxation,
no real pressures,
no unnecessary excitement.

Complete
and utter
blissful,
contentment,

which I will soon have to leave behind
when college ends and I find myself
opening the door to
the world outside . . .
. . . my bedroom door.

And it all looks rather frightening.
It's big out there . . .

I feel unprepared for what lies ahead.
I always thought that I'd feel different as
an adult.

But I don't.
I am still that child of five entering school
for the first time.

Except this school is a lot bigger,
and a lot more frightening.

Lord, have you ever been
on a fairground ride?
or done bungee jumping?

Well,
life at present is just like that moment
before the harness clamps you into the seat
and you're actually on that ride.

Before you looms what appears to be two
hundred miles of very angry metal . . .

. . . waiting . . .
. . . drooling . . .
. . . thirsty . . .

Then suddenly –
WHOOOOOOOSH! !
You're off!

But I'm not at the 'whoosh' bit yet, Lord.

And it all looks very frightening.
There are dangers out there,
  things that can take over my life –

  a career,
  a mortgage,
  a marriage,
  children?
  and a garden plot!

Lord! Is there no escape?
These are adult things,
  adult experiences!

I'm still too young!
Look at me!
I could be all of the above before I'm thirty!
I could be happily married with children,
  a house, a lovely garden
  and a next door neighbour called Gerald!

But is life really like that, Lord?
If I am here to live and to learn,
  I want to.
I want to experience what lies beyond
  my bedroom door,
  like the fairground ride.
It all looks so big,
  so terrifying;
  but once you're on
  and the excitement takes hold,
  you wonder why the thought
  of not having a go
  ever crossed your mind.

The thrills that are out there.
All the fun of the fair!
And it's free!
God given!

I *am* frightened Lord.
I really am.
But out there lies even more of the fun I've
  been having for the previous
  twenty-two years!
And if that's anything to go by
  then I want some more –

new people to meet,
new experiences to be a part of,
whole unwritten chapters of my life
just waiting to be filled in!

So Lord,
as I step on to the fairground ride of life,
and stare ahead along the tracks of
the future,
I ask of you just one small favour . . .

make sure I don't fall out . . .

Amen.